TALK TO SYBEX ONLINE.

W9-CFJ-078

12/95

JOIN THE SYBEX FORUM ON COMPUSERVE®

- Talk to SYBEX authors, editors and fellow forum members.

- Get tips, hints, and advice online.

- Download shareware and the source code from SYBEX books.

If you're already a CompuServe user, just enter GO SYBEX to join the SYBEX Forum. If you're not, try CompuServe free by calling 1-800-848-8199 and ask for Representative 560. You'll get one free month of basic service and a $15 credit for CompuServe extended services—a $23.95 value. Your personal ID number and password will be activated when you sign up.

**Join us online today. Enter GO SYBEX on CompuServe.
If you're not a CompuServe member,
call Representative 560 at 1-800-848-8199**

(outside U.S./Canada call 614-457-0802)

SYBEX
Shortcuts to
Understanding

For every kind of computer user, there is a SYBEX book.

All computer users learn in their own way. Some need straightforward and methodical explanations. Others are just too busy for this approach. But no matter what camp you fall into, SYBEX has a book that can help you get the most out of your computer and computer software while learning at your own pace.

Beginners generally want to start at the beginning. The **ABC's** series, with its step-by-step lessons in plain language, helps you build basic skills quickly. For a more personal approach, there's the **Murphy's Laws** and **Guided Tour** series. Or you might try our **Quick & Easy** series, the friendly, full-color guide, with **Quick & Easy References**, the companion pocket references to the **Quick & Easy** series. If you learn best by doing rather than reading, find out about the **Hands-On Live!** series, our new interactive multimedia training software. For hardware novices, there's the **Your First** series.

The **Mastering and Understanding** series will tell you everything you need to know about a subject. They're perfect for intermediate and advanced computer users, yet they don't make the mistake of leaving beginners behind. Add one of our **Instant References** and you'll have more than enough help when you have a question about your computer software. You may even want to check into our **Secrets & Solutions** series.

SYBEX even offers special titles on subjects that don't neatly fit a category—like our **Pushbutton Guides**, our books about the Internet, our books about the latest computer games, and a wide range of books for Macintosh computers and software.

SYBEX books are written by authors who are expert in their subjects. In fact, many make their living as professionals, consultants or teachers in the field of computer software. And their manuscripts are thoroughly reviewed by our technical and editorial staff for accuracy and ease-of-use.

So when you want answers about computers or any popular software package, just help yourself to SYBEX.

For a complete catalog of our publications, please write:

SYBEX Inc.
2021 Challenger Drive
Alameda, CA 94501
Tel: (510) 523-8233/(800) 227-2346 Telex: 336311
Fax: (510) 523-2373

SYBEX is committed to using natural resources wisely to preserve and improve our environment. As a leader in the computer book publishing industry, we are aware that over 40% of America's solid waste is paper. This is why we have been printing the text of books like this one on recycled paper since 1982.

This year our use of recycled paper will result in the saving of more than 15,300 trees. We will lower air pollution effluents by 54,000 pounds, save 6,300,000 gallons of water, and reduce landfill by 2,700 cubic yards.

In choosing a SYBEX book you are not only making a choice for the best in skills and information, you are also choosing to enhance the quality of life for all of us.

Thorne

Myst®

Strategies and Secrets

Anne Ryman

SYBEX

SAN FRANCISCO • PARIS • DÜSSELDORF • SOEST

Acquisitions Manager:
Kristine Plachy

Developmental Editor:
Gary Masters

Editor:
Dusty Bernard

Project Editor:
Kristen Vanberg-Wolff

Technical Editor:
David Hendee

Book Designers:
Pace Design Group, San Francisco

Proofreader/Production Assistant:
Dave Nash

Cover Designer:
Archer Design

Cover Illustrator:
Robert Jew

To Dad,

who has finally stopped suggesting I take accounting classes

and

To Mom,

who would have preferred a whodunnit.

Maybe next time.

Acknowledgments

As with any project of this sort, it would not have been possible to write this book without the help of many people. Thanks to Matt, who suggested me for the project in the first place; Doug, who fed me Advil when it got down to the wire; and Pat and Brian, who got married the weekend of the final deadline and made me finish the manuscript early.

Developmental editor Gary Masters was invaluable in developing the concept, and super-editor Dusty Bernard not only can *almost* read my handwriting, but also trekked through the torrential California rains to reach the FedEx drop box. In addition, Kris Vanberg-Wolff graciously answered my naive book-publishing questions, and technical editor David Hendee caught all the fibs, flubs, and fabrications. In addition, Cliff Gerrish at Pace Design Group made the graphics of *Myst* look even lovelier. The people at Cyan and Brøderbund were generous with their time and promptly returned phone calls and faxes.

And a final big "thank you" to the Coca-Cola Company for continuing to manufacture the caffeine-rich and saccharin-filled beverage Tab. Believe me, this book could not have been written without it.

— Table of Contents —

Introduction:
The *Myst* Phenomenon

Y ou can keep your flight simulators and your fantasy role-playing games—I'm a graphic-adventure fiend. I've helped Indiana Jones find Atlantis and Roger Wilco fix his spaceships. I've *Loom*-ed and *Laura Bow*-ed. I've taken a Cruise for a Corpse and helped Sam and Max Hit the Road.

Then there's *Myst*. Few games have had the word of mouth of *Myst*, and in an industry where a two-month shelf life is the norm, *Myst* has remained a bestseller for almost two years now. This game is a phenomenon in the true sense of the word: "something extraordinary, an appearance whose cause is not immediately obvious," as *Webster's* says.

If *Myst* had to rely simply on its plot and puzzles, it would have been successful, but it might never have topped the charts. The reason *Myst* has been featured in every publication from *Entertainment Weekly* to *The Wall Street Journal* is its atmosphere. The game's graphics and sound are truly astounding—all the more so now that two-, three-, and four-disk games are coming out that can't equal the beauty in *Myst's* solo CD. Game players are proving to game publishers that it takes something more than digitized graphics to win them over.

Myst's look got it publicity, and once word of mouth spread ("You *have* to see this *game!*"), the frenzy had begun. A lot of buyers had just purchased a CD-ROM drive for their Mac or PC and wanted something to show off the new technology. For some people, *Myst* was the first game they had ever bought. For others, it was their first graphic adventure. The world of *Myst* is so lovely that even when you're driven to distraction by a puzzle you can't solve, you can take a break, walk around one of the islands, and wish it were part of a Club Med package.

Only the experienced graphic-adventurers griped about *Myst*—after all, it *is* a little lonely and a little on the easy side for a veteran—but I'll bet even they will be standing in line the day *Myst II* goes on sale. No matter what people see as the game's shortcomings, everyone's gonna want to help Atrus rescue poor Catherine from the island on which she's held captive.

—*Anne Ryman*

Chapter 1

How to Myst

Look, you shelled out the money for *Myst*, and you owe it to yourself to play the game on your own. Really. Playing the game with a walk-thru is cheating. It's like reading the last page of a mystery, like having the answer key for an exam, like…. Well, you get the idea.

So the purpose of this book isn't to lead you through *Myst*—although you can certainly use it for that. But this book is to help you get past the sticky places without ripping out your hair. The clues are carefully arranged, so once you have the information you need, you can put down the book and get on with the game. For example, say there's a blue bottle on a shelf you can't reach. The text under "Blue Bottle" isn't going to begin: "Get the blue bottle by knocking out the shelf support with a broom." It will start out by pointing you in the right direction: "You can't climb up to the blue bottle, so look for a way to make it come to you." Then, if you continue reading, you'll find out where to find the broom and which notch to hit. Get the picture? It's subtle-like.

And if you really don't want to take the chance that you'll see something you don't want to see, check out the "Quick Fix to Tricky Bits" questions at the end of each chapter. These are answers to the most common problems in each area and can quickly point you in the right direction.

— Getting Technical —

Myst is available for both PC and Macintosh computers, and the game play is virtually identical for both. (Notice is made in the text whenever there are differences.) It's also pretty close to a "plug-and-play" game—there aren't any fancy instructions to follow, and even novices shouldn't get tripped up. If you *are* having problems, check out the appendices in the back of this book, where the technical support guys for *Myst* supply solutions to the problems that occur most often.

Myst runs under Windows for PC users; the game requires a 386 computer but runs best on a 486. You must also have 4MB of RAM, 4MB of free space on your hard drive, Super VGA graphics, Windows 3.1, DOS 5.0 or higher, and a mouse. All of this equipment is fairly standard on any computer with a CD-ROM drive.

Go into Windows and select Run, then Browse for your CD-ROM drive. Double-click on the INSTALL.EXE command; sit back and watch the magic. The program asks you on which drive you wish the game installed and what you wish to call the file; default commands install C:\MYST. Once the game is installed, double-click the Myst icon, and you're off and running.

Mac players need a 256-color Macintosh, 4MB of RAM, 2500K of free RAM, a 7.0.1 system or higher, QuickTime 1.6, Sound Manager 3.0, and 3MB of hard-disk space. You must install both QuickTime and Sound Manager before playing by dragging them from the *Myst* CD into the system folder on your hard drive; reboot your computer after they're installed. You must also turn off System 7's Virtual Memory from the Memory control panel. Again, reboot after you've turned it off.

Copy the Myst icon and file folders (called Myst Files) from the CD to any location you wish on your hard drive; then double-click the Myst icon to begin the adventure.

Slowdowns occasionally occur in *Myst,* when it can take forever to access the simplest commands. This means your memory is dangerously low (as the screen probably tells you). Find a good place to save your game, exit, then restart the adventure. You can avoid some slowdowns by closing any screen savers or other unnecessary utilities.

A quick word about the game's interface: you can play *Myst* in three ways. The default interface jumps from board to board so you see all the scenery and all the stairs and all the corners. There's also a Transition mode that gently fades the different boards into view. And finally, there's the Zip mode, which uses the same jump interface as with the default but skips a few steps for places you've already explored whenever it's applicable.

You should use either the Default or Transition mode for initial exploration, but the Zip mode (indicated

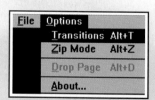

Select the interface you want from this menu.

by a lightning-bolt cursor) is particularly handy once you know your way around or when you're making return visits to one of the Ages.

A quick word as well about *Myst*'s save-game feature. For some reason known only to its designers, you can save the game whenever you want, but restored games perversely place you in one of two spots—either in the library on Myst Island or at the beginning of whatever Age you're visiting. Therefore, there's a certain strategy involved in saving your games so you don't end up backtracking any more than necessary.

First of all, always save your game the minute you land in a new Age and the minute you return to the library. Realize that if, for example, you've rotated a fortress into position and saved your game for the evening, the fortress will be in its original location when you return the next day. This can be infuriating during tricky parts of the game, but sometimes another ten minutes of game play can solve the problem. Occasionally—*very* occasionally—the save-game feature can actually be a boon. If you've got an item you need and don't want to trace your steps all the way back to, say, ground level, you can save your game, restore it, and be back at the beginning—at ground level.

— Guidelines to — Graphic Adventures

If you've played any graphic adventures at all, you know the Cardinal Rules of Adventuring:

1. Save, and save often.

2. Explore every nook and cranny.

3. Keep track of all the clues.

Now, the save-game part isn't as important in *Myst* because you can't die. You can't walk off cliffs, drown in rising waters, or impale yourself on spikes. However, as noted, the restore-game feature stinks, so don't forget to save your game a couple of times during each Age and immediately upon your return to Myst Island. Save these versions of the game as separate files so you don't have far to backtrack if you overlook something or get lost.

Exploring is also easier in *Myst* than in most graphic adventures because you don't have to worry about building your inventory. With few exceptions, the only things you can pick up in *Myst* are the red and blue pages that help unravel the plot. Since there's no inventory screen, you can carry only one thing at a time; pick up an additional item, and the one you're already holding goes back to its original location. So when you find something you want to hang onto, just remember the location of additional items. Again, this really comes into play only with the red and blue pages; even if you're holding one of these pages, you can still, for example, read a note found in a drawer, use a key, or control a lever or switch.

The levers and switches bring us to a different problem: to turn on or not to turn on? Personally, I tend not to push every button or switch I find until I've done a lot of exploring. This is a habit born of many unsatisfying deaths in other graphic adventures. (You never know which button is going to fry you in your tracks.) Since you can't die in *Myst*, you don't lose anything by flipping every handle you see, but you might not find out what the different switches are for, either. Truly strategic minds might try exploring thoroughly, noting the location of similar-looking or similarly placed switches and then turning on *one* to see what happens.

Control panels are usually a different case. Most of those in *Myst* require specific data entries; you can fool around 'til Doomsday and not hit the right combo. It's better just to find the correct formula, symbol, or number, then proceed.

And keeping track of all the clues? Well, that's where this book comes in. All the notes, clues, and hints are in here, conveniently located right where you need them. So don't even bother to sharpen your pencil, pal—you won't be needing it. You can use that big *Myst Journal* that comes with the game for phone messages from people trying to distract you from the business at hand.

Getting Around *Myst*

The simple interface in *Myst* means there are a lot of places you want to go that you can't, but it also means that it's hard to overlook places you *need* to go. The rule of thumb is to look in all four directions (or, frequently, only two) whenever you enter a room or a new location. Take a look at all the switches or posted directions on the walls; these are usually located near doorways. If you don't know how to use one, just remember what it looks like and where it's located. You can always come back later.

You're going to see a lot of symbols, maps, and clues scattered around. Again, this book keeps track of all of those so you don't *need* to note them yourself. But if you're trying to play the game on your own, jot them down in that *Myst Journal* alongside your phone messages. Look very, very closely; some buttons are a mere pixel on the screen. If you're stuck, you could easily have missed something, so try a little more close observation and random clicking.

The plot of *Myst* isn't immediately apparent. In fact, you get only bits and pieces of it as you advance through the game. So you also might want to keep tabs on the snatches of dialog you hear, and maybe even the attitude or demeanor of the person talking to you. Not that you meet too many people. *Myst*ing is a fairly lonely experience.

You visit four islands in addition to Myst Island. Each of these Ages is self contained—you don't need anything from the Mechanical Age to solve the Stoneship Age, for instance. This means you can visit the different Ages in any order you like, and if you're having trouble solving one, you can return to Myst Island and try someplace else. This book visits the Ages in alphabetical order for no reason whatsoever except to show that you can, indeed, visit the Ages in any order you'd like.

The object in each Age is to find the red and blue pages required by the books in the library—they're the only way you're going to figure out what's going on. As you return each page, the men trapped in the books give you hints about what's caused their imprisonment. The pages aren't different for each Age; instead, you get the same conversation for the first page you return, the second page, and so on, no matter where you found those pages. Get it? Good.

Chapter 2

In the Mood

Myst is really an incredible land, and you owe it to yourself to take the game slowly. Your first visit to Myst Island is gonna be spent ooo-ing and ahh-ing at the gorgeous scenery and mood-setting sound. Accept the fact that you're not going to know what's going on at first—Who's that guy falling through space? Who am I supposed to be? What's going *on?*—and take a little walk around.

This is your chance to explore o'plenty, and it's the first thing you should do on any island or Age you reach.

The Dock

From your position on the dock—let's assume you're heading north—you can hear the tide gently lapping the pier and almost feel the warm rays of the sun. It's a perfect day for a boat ride, but the only vessel in sight is the sunken ship to your right, its mast and crow's nest just visible above the clear blue waters of Myst Island.

To your left the breezy atmosphere changes. There's a door cut into the mountainside and a dark and foreboding staircase leading down to—believe it or not—a bubbling cauldron. Is this *Myst*...or *Macbeth*?

Back on the dock there's a large switch inset on a podium. You see more of them as you explore the island.

A door to your left leads down to a mysterious cauldron filled with water. Push the button and watch strange gears appear.

~ The Giant Cog ~

S traight ahead from the dock is the highest point on Myst Island you can initially reach. You can't move around the giant cog, but take a gander at that view! If you look to one side and directly up, you see a mountain tower stretching toward the clouds. Slightly to one side is a good view of an impressive granite rotunda that looks like your next stop.

~ The Planetarium ~

M ount the stairs toward the buildings in the center of the island. For now, disregard the note lying on the ground—we'll get to that later. If you open the door to the first building, you catch a glimpse of what looks like a dentist's chair. But when you sit down in the chair, you see that there's a strange instrument above you with data-entry buttons. Maybe it's just too bright inside to see what's going on. Climb down from the chair and click off the light switch at the door. Aha! Now the dome is covered with stars. The instrument would seem to indicate specific constellations…if only you knew the correct information to enter.

─ The Library ─

Just beyond the planetarium is a large columned building that—judging from its books and maps—would seem to be the library. This building is the heart and soul of *Myst,* both the island and the game. Take a look around, but leave a full inventory until you've finished exploring the island.

─ The Rocket ─

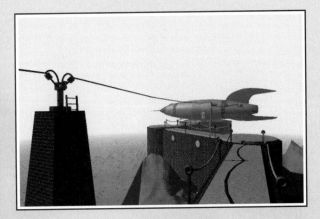

Behind the library and accessible only by a concrete walkway built along the far coast of Myst Island is a curious rocketship that looks like it has been patterned out of something by Jules Verne or H.G. Wells. Go ahead and take a look inside— the power supply seems to have something to do with that organ, a strange addition for a spacecraft.

You should also notice that the rocketship is connected to a stone building barely visible through the trees by a series of power lines. Who needs polluting fuel when you've got good old electricity?

~ The Fountain ~

There's a dry fountain south of the rocket and the library, and a ship's model that would seem to match the one on Myst Island lies deep inside. The picturesque fountain is located on the outskirts of the woods that cover the southern tip of Myst Island, and the fountain is also surrounded by pillars. Taking a close look at one of them, you see an emblem with a small button beneath it. The symbols must be a clue to getting the fountain running again.

The fountain houses a sunken ship that seems modeled after the one on the dock. Strange symbols surround the fountain, but nothing happens when you push the buttons under them.

~ The Generator Shed ~

The path below the fountain takes you farther into the sun-dappled woods, and for the first time, you hear some signs of life—even if it is only the chirping of local birds. You see a shed to your right with stairs leading underground. Follow them to a door that opens at your touch. It leads to the controls of the generator. As you experiment with

the series of buttons on the control panel, power surges are indicated by the two large dials on the left. Finally, one of the dials falls back to zero…another clue that will be explained later. The diagram near the exit doesn't cast much, uh, light on the subject.

‒ The Cabin ‒

A log cabin lies almost directly opposite the generator shed, a cozy home in the thick of the woods. But there's no comfortable furniture or snug fireplace inside. Instead, the far wall is dominated by a furnace, and there's a locked safe on the wall near the door.

If you take a walk just behind the cabin, you'll see what the large diagram of the tree inside indicated. A brick wall surrounds the massive tree you find, but there seems to be no way to scale the towering trunk.

‒ The Clock Tower ‒

There's a final stop to make on your exploration, but there's not that much left to see. The charming clock tower on the far tip of Myst Island would be a nice place to visit…if only you had remembered to bring your water wings. As it is, the tower is far enough from the mainland to make it inaccessible. Again, a control panel is clearly in view, but nothing seems to happen as you experiment with it.

Now that you've got your bearings, it's time to get down to the serious matter of game play. The secrets of *Myst* await.

Chapter 3

Myst Island

The story line for *Myst* is as nebulous as the fog swirling around Myst Island. As the game begins, a man is seen falling through space; then you focus on the book of Myst. Opening it, you see a view screen with an overhead perspective of the island. Click on that window, and you land on Myst.

Myst Island

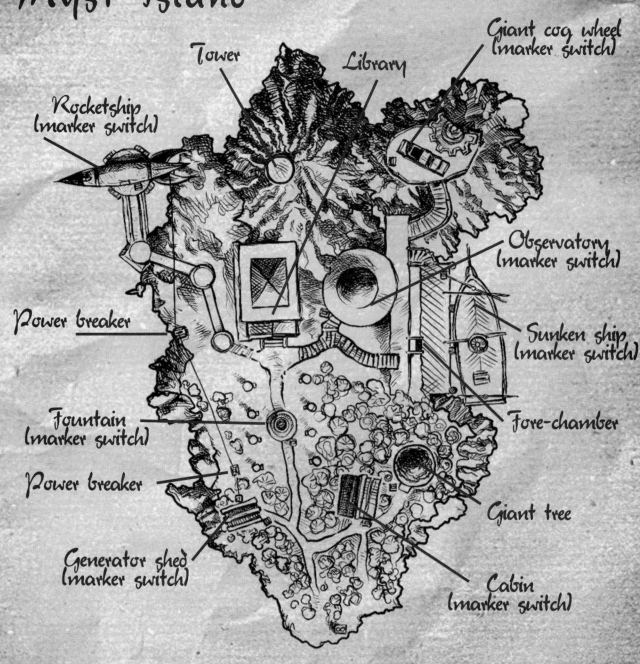

Rocketship
(marker switch)

Tower

Library

Giant cog wheel
(marker switch)

Observatory
(marker switch)

Power breaker

Sunken ship
(marker switch)

Fore-chamber

Fountain
(marker switch)

Power breaker

Giant tree

Generator shed
(marker switch)

Cabin
(marker switch)

Clock tower
(marker switch)

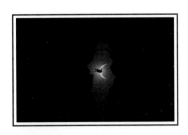

Pick yourself up, dust yourself off, and take a look around. You seem to be on a dock. To your right is a

sunken ship. To your left is a doorway. There's a stairway up ahead and nothing behind you. What to do, what to do….

First of all, get your bearings. If you walk straight ahead and up the stairs, you can continue straight toward a giant cog wheel, or veer left and continue up the path toward the buildings you see in the distance. What's that lying in the grass? Aha! Clue #1, a mysterious note.

Catherine,
I've left for you a message of utmost importance in our fore-chamber beside the dock. Enter the number of marker switches on this island into the imager to retrieve the message.

Yours,
Atrus

Okay, that note explains those mysterious switches you've seen around the island. So now while you explore, note the location of each marker switch. And that room back on the dock must lead to the fore-chamber. Maybe you should backtrack to the dock and take a closer look.

The Fore-Chamber

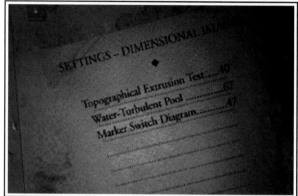

Moving down the stairs and through a hallway, you spot a cauldron in the middle of a dark room. You look into the waters, press the button, and catch a brief glimpse of some underlying machinery before the waters rise once again. Hmm. Looking around the room, you spot a sign on the wall by the door: Settings—Dimensional Imager.

There's a tiny green button in the upper left-hand corner. Push it, and a control panel appears. Here's your chance to enter the number settings.

Topographical Extrusion Test

That's the second reference to marker switches, so that must be your next step: find all the marker switches and turn them all on. The switches turn out to be as handy as a trail of bread-crumbs…. While looking for them, you end up explor-ing the rest of the island and uncover more of its secrets.

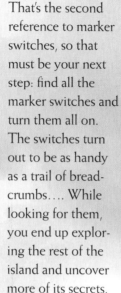

Water Turbulent Pool

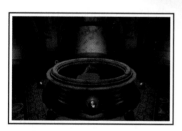

Marker Switch Diagram

Using the dock as the easternmost point, there are two switches on the east side of Myst Island, two on the west, and the rest more or less in a strip down the center of the island. You won't be able to reach one of them yet, but don't let that bother you.

— The Master Switches —

Now that you know how many switches there are, ignore the call of the library for just another moment or two and go back to the fore-chamber. Enter the number of switches in the control panel and get your first message from Atrus.

The explorer's message is again to his wife, Catherine. Something has obviously gone horribly wrong on Myst Island. Most of his books have been burned, and he suspects one of his sons is responsible. Before he leaves the island, however, Atrus reminds Catherine about the "tower rotation." The plot thickens.

— The Library —

Where else would you go for research? There's a reason all the paths on Myst Island lead to the library. Now that you've got a vague idea of what's going on, trek up the hill once more and explore the library's secrets.

When you search the bookshelf, however, you find that most of the books have been burnt beyond salvation. Read the volumes you can; their information is invaluable. In addition to providing you with maps of the Ages

that Atrus has explored, they give you more insight into Atrus's plans and how his sons, Sirrus and Achenar, came to be with him while his wife stayed behind. In addition, you first hear of the magical places—Everdunes, Stoneship, Selenitic—that you soon will be visiting. There's also a puzzle book on the shelves; don't bother to copy the grids. (There are 300 of them!) Just remember the book is there.

Two books, one red and one blue, have been set apart from those on the library shelves. When you open the volumes, you get static-filled reception. From the red book, a man identifies himself as Sirrus and high-handedly demands that you bring him more red pages. The man in the blue book seems slightly unbalanced as he, too, commands you to bring him pages for his blue book.

Sirrus inhabits the red book (top). The image in the blue book is his brother, Achenar (bottom).

Another wall in the library houses an enormous fireplace. You can walk inside and see the button on the inside wall, but nothing happens when you push it. Don't worry—its secrets will be revealed in due time.

The map on one wall appears to be Myst Island. All the objects with marker switches are indicated (as long as you've turned on the switches). There's a round tower in back of the library that's blinking. When you press it, "Tower Rotation" appears at the bottom of the map, and you hear the sound of machinery. The line moves only a fraction of an inch, however, so press the tower again and hold down.

Notice that the indicator line turns red at four different locations: the giant cog wheel, the sunken ship, the giant tree, and the rocketship.

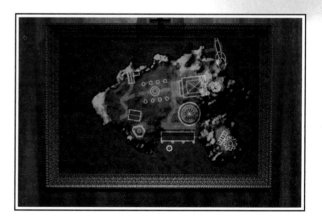

The final objects in the library are two paintings, each featuring almost exactly the same scene: the library door either opened or closed. Click on the "closed" painting, and suddenly a secret passageway is revealed behind the bookcase.

Walk down the passageway until you reach an elevator. There's a switch inside that indicates the library level. Push the switch, and the elevator takes you to the tower.

A ladder comes into view as the elevator door opens. It has a book emblem between two rungs. Climb up to the observatory, and you can see the island. If you left the map downstairs so that the tower indicator line was red, you should see the item the red line pointed to from the observatory. Otherwise, you'll just get a lovely view of the mist.

Climb the "Book" ladder for a view of an object on the island; then climb the "Key" ladder behind the elevator for a vital clue about that location.

If you have one of the four points in view, take a look around the elevator shaft. There's something out of view that's key to getting anywhere in *Myst*— literally. A matching ladder, this one with a key emblem on it, lies opposite the book ladder. Climb up until you see a clue that corresponds with the object seen from the book ladder.

So now you've got the clues you need to travel to the other Ages…but getting to them is going to be half the battle.

Quick Fix for Tricky Bits

What the heck am I supposed to do? I'm just wandering around aimlessly.

Get your bearings, then start turning on the marker switches. Enter the total number of switches into the dimensional imager control box.

The map of Myst Island in the library is incomplete!

You've missed a marker switch somewhere. Make sure all the switches you can reach are turned on, then go back to the map.

I can't get the tower to rotate. How come?

You need to press and *hold* the tower indicator on the map. Stop whenever the rotation line turns red.

Where are the clues to the Ages that I'm supposed to find? I just don't get it.

You're missing a vital clue in the tower. There are *two* ladders inside, one clearly visible and the other hidden behind the elevator. Use the tower rotation in combination with the two ladders to get the four clues you need.

I saw the clues, but I was incredibly stupid and didn't write them down. Save me some time and tell me what they are.

Sunken ship:	October 11, 1984, 10:04 a.m.
	January 17, 1207, 5:46 a.m.
	November 23, 9791, 6:57 p.m.
Giant cog wheel:	2:40, 2, 2, 1
Rocketship:	59 volts
Tree:	7, 2, 4

Chapter 4

Channelwood Age

T he journals in the library describe Channelwood as a place where water covers the land as far as you can see, except for a small rocky island. Trees grow directly out of the water, and the only way to get around is on wooden platforms.

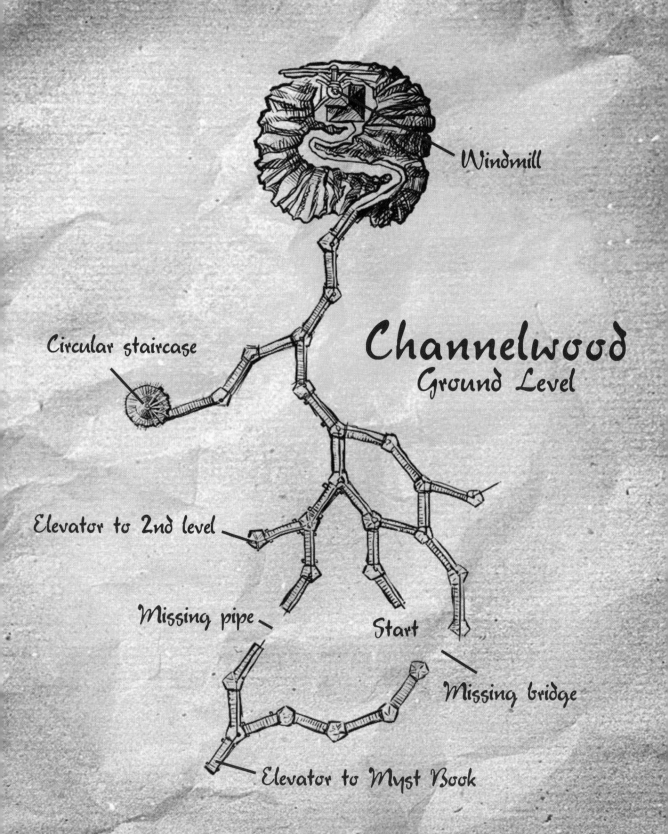

Windmill

Circular staircase

Channelwood
Ground Level

Elevator to 2nd level

Missing pipe

Start

Missing bridge

Elevator to Myst Book

Channelwood was once a huge island on which humans and monkey-like creatures lived in harmony—the humans on the ground and the monkey-like creatures in treetop villages. But a catastrophic earthquake or volcano struck the island, and much of it sank beneath the water. Those humans who survived moved into the tree village, but most quickly died.

By the time Atrus visited Channelwood, only one human was left—a gray-haired man who was treated as a god by the monkey creatures. But after imparting the history of the island to Atrus, he said to the traveler, "We had expected you to come sooner," then he walked off a platform to his death. The monkey creatures burned the old man on a funeral pyre and transferred their adoration to Atrus.

Atrus brought his sons to stay with him on Channelwood, but Catherine refused to join them. After a long visit, he left the boys behind at their own request and resumed his own travels.

Getting There

The tower clues point to the tree and to the numbers 7, 2, 4.

How better to get to a village in the trees than via Myst Island's own towering trunk? The tower clue for the Channelwood Age is 7, 2, 4 —the safe combination for the cabin in the woods.

Go to the cabin and enter the combination, then open the safe. There's only a box of matches inside,

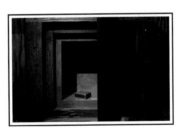

but how else did you expect to fire up the furnace that dominates the far wall of the cabin?

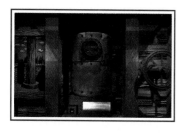 Take a look at the furnace. There's a small square in the lower left-hand corner. That's the pilot light. Touch it with the lit match, and you're ready to roll. Now turn the power wheel clockwise (indicated by green arrows) as far as you can. The furnace blasts into overdrive, and in a few minutes you hear a BANG-BANG-BANG noise from outside.

Quickly run outside and look at the big tree. There's an elevator pounding its way to the top. Once it reaches the treetop, however, it stops. Go back inside, turn off the power wheel (red arrows), and listen as the elevator drops back down. When you go back outside, you'll see that it didn't conveniently stop at ground level, but continued underground. Since there's no platform at the top of the tree, you must need to be in the elevator car as it goes back underground. (You can take the elevator up for a lovely island view, then press a button to release the steam to go back to ground—but not underground—level.)

Go back inside the cabin and power up the furnace again. Listen for the elevator car to reach the top of the tree and turn off the power. Run outside again and hop into the elevator car before it disappears. The Myst book is in the chamber down below. Click on it, and you're on your way.

— Take a Look Around —

D on't forget to save your game as soon as
you reach this, or any other, Age. It's very
easy to find your way around the "ground"
level of Channelwood; there are a few landmarks
that help you get your bearings as you explore the
winding wooden platforms, all of which are connected by great stretches of pipe. The first thing you'll
notice is several wooden elevators, although none of
them seems to work. You can see the outlines of
structures built in the trees; these elevators must take
you to them.

There's also a gap
in a platform with a
lever nearby and
another gap where
the pipeline sud-
denly ends. There's
another elevator
beyond the gap
that you can't yet
reach. Behind you,
you can barely see
a windmill on a
rocky outcropping
to the far left of
your starting posi-
tion. Since that's
the only power
source in sight, it
must be where your
mission begins.

**The landmarks you should
spot on Channelwood are a
simple elevator, an elevator alongside a circular
staircase, and a windmill.**

**Other sites to mark
are the point at
which a walkway
suddenly ends and
another spot
where a section of
pipe is missing.**

Getting Down to Business

Bear left from your starting position and work your way over to the windmill. Climb up the hill to the structure and go inside. There you see a large water tank on the right and hear the trickle of water from a leak to your left. A  small faucet is located near the base of the tank; turn it and you hear water running into the pipeline. Now Channelwood has power.

As you're walking back toward the heart of Channelwood, notice the pipeline that runs above the walkways. There's a plate-like switch highlighted by yellow dots located where certain walkways branch out.

Those are the water mains by which you control the water pressure leaving the windmill. By moving the switch left or right, you control the direction in which the water flows. It takes all the pressure possible to get the elevators to work, but it's very easy to guide the water in the direction you wish—the water flows in the direction of the yellow dots.

The circular stairs are blocked by a locked door—for now. You must access the treetop village from the other elevator. Move the switches so that the water flows directly to the elevator, then step inside, close the door, and pull down the lever to go up one level.

You quickly see that this village consists of a series of wooden huts connected by rope-and-plank ladders. You also realize that the layout is somewhat familiar—it's the same drawing Atrus drew in his journal!

Channelwood
Second Level

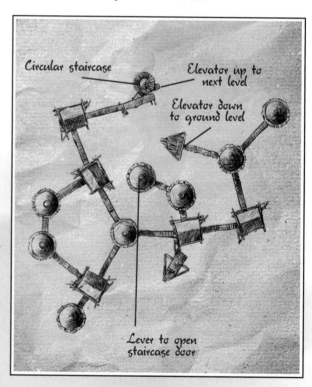

It's a simple matter to flip a few switches, climb the staircase again, and ride the newly powered elevator one more level upward. And there's not much left to explore—just the playground of Sirrus and Achenar.

Achenar's room is located straight ahead from the elevator platform. But there's another room in between…a strange room in which a holographic image of Achenar speaks to you in an unknown tongue. This is perhaps the language of the monkey-like creatures; Atrus said in his journals that the brothers were learning the dialect.

It can be hard to find your way around the treetop village because all the buildings basically look alike, and the interface won't let you look around to get your bearings. Your purpose on this level is to access the circular staircase. Somewhere in these huts is a lever that opens that locked staircase door. From your position from the elevator that brought you up to this level, go straight into the first hut, then work your way to the right. The lever is located in the dead-end hut you eventually reach. Don't see it? Look to the right under a window. As you approach the lever, you can see the circular staircase from the window; pull the lever, and the door opens.

Now leave the hut and continue moving to the right until you reach the circular staircase and the elevator. Try the elevator? No luck, of course—the water pressure is still powering the other elevator. You need to climb down the staircase and reroute the water so it's powering this elevator.

Achenar's bedroom is furnished with only a rough-hewn bed, stark lighting, and a bizarre video machine that's located in one corner along with a blue page from his book. The machine has four buttons. The first three bring up images of Achenar, looking very unbalanced and speaking in that bizarre language again. But Sirrus appears when you push the fourth button, deriding his brother by "hoping he didn't erase anything" when he tried out the machine.

Stopping back at the room in the middle, you get an image of Sirrus this time. And stand back when you press those buttons—the brothers evidently have a warped sense of humor.

Sirrus's bedroom is hidden in back of the elevator, but you spot it as you retrace your steps. His surroundings look even more opulent in contrast to Achenar's rustic bedroom. The bed is elaborately carved, but several chairs have been broken—in a fit of rage?

Two drawers are built into the base of Sirrus's bed. The left-hand drawer reveals a dagger with a wickedly sharp edge. Amidst the wine bottles in the second drawer is a torn note. You can read only half:

ch Vault Access
and of Myst

ated in very plain view on
Myst, and access can be
easily if the simple
ollowed. First, locate
Switches on the island.
these switches to the
en go to the dock and,
rn the Marker Switch
e "off" position.

This note obviously refers to something back on Myst—a secret vault? And it looks like those marker switches are going to come into play again.

Continuing your search of the room, you uncover only one more item, a red page hidden in Sirrus's desk. Take either the red or blue page with you; return for the other once you've discovered a way back to Myst Island.

With a new page in your sweaty little hand, it's time to make tracks back to the library to see what it reveals. Access must lie with that elevator beyond the gaps in the walkway and pipeline. Work your way over to where the walkway ends. There's a lever just to the left. If you switch the direction of the water pressure, a hidden segment of walkway appears; it won't sink back underwater even if you change the pipeline pressure.

What works in one place will work in another. Cross the new bridge and work your way over to the elevator. There's a crank located by the pipe; turn it, and it extends across the gap. Now it's a simple case of retracing your steps and putting the water

pressure through this pipeline. Hop in the elevator, and it takes you upward to a secret chamber where—you guessed it!—a Myst book waits to take you back to Myst Island.

— The Pages —

The first two pages of the blue and red books confirm your initial impression of the brothers. Achenar seems unhinged, while Sirrus is cool but arrogant.

As you listen to the blue page transmission—which is still filled with static—Achenar accuses his brother of being an egotistical fool and a liar. He claims he has been falsely imprisoned. "Don't listen to him.... I will have my retribution!" he screams.

Sirrus is much calmer as he tries to convince you that he has been wrongfully imprisoned and that Achenar is guilty. It's hard to tell who to trust at this early stage in the game. Neither seems like the trustworthy companion you need for a journey such as this. Maybe the next pages will help you see the brothers' true colors.

Quick Fix for Tricky Bits

I've got a match in hand, but I can't light the furnace.

You've got a match—but is it a *lit* match? Strike it against the box before moving to the furnace.

I can't get any of the elevators to run.

Water pressure is the key to power on Channelwood. Open the faucet at the base of the water tank inside the windmill, then direct the water with the plate switches in the direction you wish it to go.

How do I open the door at the top of the circular staircase?

There's a lever in one of the huts— pull it, and the door opens.

I can't find Sirrus's bedroom.

If you turn to your left as you leave the elevator on the third level, you'll see the walkway to Sirrus's room. It's more visible if you're walking back from Achenar's bedroom toward the elevator.

Chapter 5

Mechanical Age

Atrus describes the Mechanical Age as a dark, gray land where lightning constantly streaks across the sky. When he visited the Age, he was greeted by an old man with a beard and hair down to his waist. The elderly inhabitant told Atrus the story of the Age: it had once been a beautiful city rising from the water, surrounded by three high hills. Its people had no way of traveling across the water.

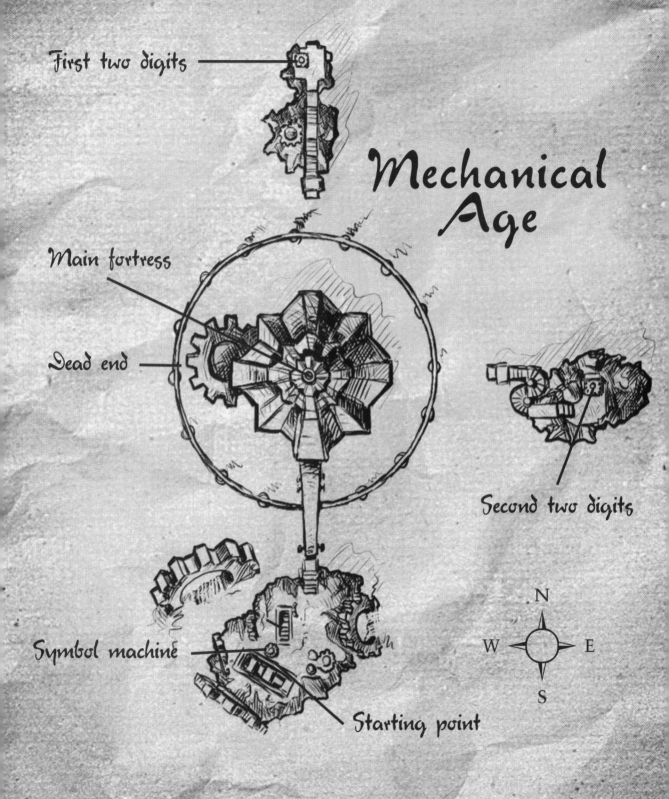

First two digits

Mechanical Age

Main fortress

Dead end

Second two digits

Symbol machine

Starting point

N
W · E
S

One day guards on a lookout post located on the eastern hill spotted black ships on the horizon. The sentries were quickly overwhelmed by the invaders, who razed the land, then sailed away. Only eight survived, and two of those people soon died.

All this took place nine years before Atrus arrived in the Age, but it is rumored the black ships will return in another year. Atrus set upon a plan so those in the Mechanical Age could resist the next attack. He brought his sons, Sirrus and Achenar, to the Age, and together all the inhabitants began building a fortress on the foundations of the old city.

Atrus also began experimenting with holography, and he built a device in the center of the fortress that

enabled the inhabitants to learn to use the fortress defensively in case of an attack. His plans all worked seamlessly; when the invaders returned, they were routed and sent on their way.

⁓ Getting There ⁓

Mechanical? Gears, wires, bolts—cogs! The giant cog is the key to traveling to the Mechanical Age. Do your little tower trick: rotate the map until the line turns red as it points to the cog. Then take the elevator to the tower.

The "Book" ladder gives you a view of the cog, and the "Key" ladder provides the hint—2:40 and 2-2-1.

Using the big wheel/ big hand, little wheel/ little hand analogy, it's easy enough to set the clock to 2:40. Lo and behold, a bridge made of gears rises from beneath the water, giving you access to the tower.

Cross the bridge and enter the clock tower, not forgetting to

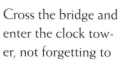

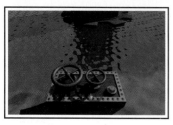

There's only one place on the island where time is important, and that's down by the clock tower. Go down and examine the wheels on the shore once again. Turn them. Nothing seems to happen. But look up at the tower again—the hands of the clock have turned!

turn on the final marker switch on your way inside.

There's not much inside except some strange machinery, with three dials with numbers on the top and two levers in the middle, one on either side. At the base of the machine is a smaller version of Myst Island's giant cog. A large lever is mounted on the wall behind the machine. The numbers on the dial read 3-3-3.

Give either lever on the machine an experimental pull, and you'll see that they control the dials at the top of the machine. The left-hand lever controls the middle and bottom dial; the right-hand lever, the middle and top dial. The lever on the wall resets the puzzle.

With a little more trial and error, you'll see that the amount of time you hold down each lever also controls how the numbers advance. If you pull and release the left lever, the middle and bottom numbers move one digit. If you *hold* the left lever, the bottom number moves by one digit, but the middle number continues moving. The same is true of the right lever: pull and release it, and the top and middle numbers advance by one. Hold it down, and the top number moves by one and the middle number continues clicking.

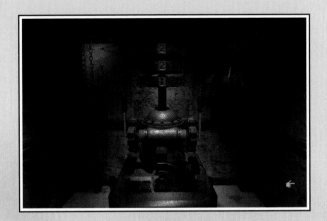

Here's one possible solution. (There are obviously several ways to get the correct answer, as is typical of *Myst* and a relief to the player.) Pull and release the left lever so the numbers move to 3-1-1. Pull and release the right lever and the numbers change to 1-2-1. Now pull and hold the right lever so the number at the top moves to the 2 position—but keep holding down until the middle number clicks to 2. When the numbers read 2-2-1 (as indicated by the tower clue), the cog at the base of the machine opens up.

Leave the clock tower and cross the island to the giant cog, and you'll see that it, too, has opened. Inside is the Myst book, your transportation to the Mechanical Age.

— Take a Look Around —

Two hallways immediately branch from the entry-way to the fortress. Both lead down to living rooms—one filled with paintings and treasures, the other with weapons and torture devices. Between these rooms there's another corridor; a red button and a small passageway break up the monotony of the iron walls.

There's a chamber at the end of that short hall, but there doesn't seem to be any way to enter, although you can see some sort of outside reflection in it. If you push the red button in the main hallway, the floor to the short passageway drops down, leading to a room that seems to be the mechanical heart of the fortress.

You can't see much from your arrival position. It's foggy, and the machinery-covered rock on which you're standing is surrounded by water. To the right, you can see another rock on which some type of structure has been built. Is that the lookout tower about which Atrus wrote? A short metal platform in front of you is surrounded by bars but doesn't lead anywhere. It's evidently controlled by a machine on a post. You get different symbols when you push the buttons on top of the machine, but nothing happens when you push the large control button.

In front of you lies a fortress rising from the sea on a circle of girders and gears. There isn't anywhere else to go, so enter the fortress.

Getting Down to Business

From your starting position, cross the walkway leading to the fortress, then choose either of the brothers' rooms to explore. Sirrus's room is even more sumptuous than his bedroom in the Channelwood Age. It's filled with paintings, fine furniture, a telescope, and a mechanical bird. There are also interesting models of some of the landmarks back on Myst Island.

As you're examining the things on Sirrus's dresser, look at the lower right-hand corner of the screen. A panel cut into the wall is half hidden by a tapestry hanging on the wall. Touch the panel, and you can scoot into the secret room it conceals.

Inside the hidden room, there's more evidence of the high-living lifestyle Sirrus enjoys. Gold and silver coins litter the floor among stacks of wooden chests, and a wine rack is filled with bottles. There's also a note in one of the wine-rack slots. It reads:

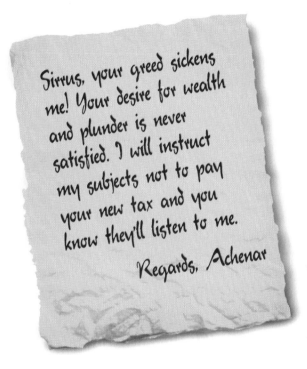

Sirrus, your greed sickens me! Your desire for wealth and plunder is never satisfied. I will instruct my subjects not to pay your new tax and you know they'll listen to me.

Regards, Achenar

A red page can also be found in the room, lying in one of the chests.

While Sirrus is obviously emerging as a greedy individual, Achenar's room does nothing to dissuade your impression of someone who's mentally unbalanced. The room is filled with weapons—normal maces, swords, and axes, but also more fiendish "toys" such as a mechanical cobra. What can only be described as a throne dominates one wall.

One interesting instrument doesn't match the rest of the decor. When you activate the machine, you get a hologram of the fortress that dissolves into a round diagram of the building. This is the holographic device Atrus constructed to teach the inhabitants of the Mechanical Age how to rotate the fortress. You, too, can practice working the levers to learn its secrets.

Note

Here's a tip you may not need at all. I played the MPC version of *Myst,* and the holographic imager caused one of the biggest problems. Every time I tried to rotate the fortress, the access times became so immense that I had to exit and start over again from a restored game. Slowdown isn't an uncommon problem, but nothing seemed to help me out, and I finally gave up trying to practice the fortress rotation. So don't worry if this happens to you. There's a key to rotating the fortress that you can learn through just a little bit of trial and error.

The objects inside the secret room include a chopping block and an axe, an electrified cage, and a mummified head in a chest. Achenar's habits are evidently very strange indeed. The shelf in one corner might help explain why he seems so erratic—it's filled with bottles of powders and potions. Maybe this brother looks for artificial means to find the pleasure Sirrus finds in material goods. By the way, don't overlook the blue page on this shelf.

Naturally, if there's a secret panel in Sirrus's room, there's bound to be a matching one in Achenar's. Look over in the corner between the holographic imager and the throne to find the hidden passage. Touch the panel, and you can move inside.

Now that you've explored this part of the fortress, it's time to rotate the building to other locations. Move to the passageway between the brothers' rooms and push the red button. Go down into the machinery room and take a closer look at the controls. If you move the lever, the two circles on the diagram come into alignment and turn red. Leave the machinery in that position and go back upstairs.

Notice that the image in the chamber across the passageway now has a woody appearance instead of showing a reflection. Push the red button to extend the walkway, step inside the chamber, and you see elevator controls to your left. Push up, and away you go.

When you reach the top of the elevator shaft, you find yourself in a room that contains little except the elevator shaft. But there's something strange about the elevator car; it has an indicator arrow pointing upward. And when you look up, you see controls on top of the elevator car.

Move back inside the elevator and press the rectangular button between the up and down arrows. You hear an alarm, and lights begin flashing. Immediately exit the car again and watch as the elevator drops down far enough to give you access to the controls.

Now comes the fun part—rotating the fortress. As promised, a neat trick to the rotation makes everything fairly easy. The fortress can be rotated into four different positions. One gives you access to the cog from which you arrived on the island. Two others lead you to symbols you need for the machine by that cog. And a fourth is a dead end. Each one of these four locations has been assigned a particular noise, and that's what you could practice learning on the holographic imager. When you've moved the levers correctly, you hear the noise. If you don't hear anything, then you've rotated the fortress into an invalid position.

A "dink" sound leads you north to the first two symbols you need.

Okay, describing noises is extremely subjective, but you should be able to make the connection with these characterizations. The noise for the initial southern position—the one you're in at this point—is a "clang" like a spoon hitting the bottom of a metal pot. For the dead-end position to the west, listen for the "swoosh" that spaceship doors make in every recent science-fiction movie. For the first two symbols' location north of your position, listen for a "dink," like those little service bells at hotel desks. And finally, the noise for the last two symbols to the east is the hardest to describe; it's a "dwip" sort of squishy noise. (Someone else described it as a "twrr," but it didn't sound anything like that to me.) You'll probably come up with your own definitions, and jot them down when you do. You'll need them in another Age.

The "swoosh" to the west is a dead end.

Follow the "dwip" or "twrr" east to the last two symbols.

The other key to rotating the fortress is the length of time you push the right-hand lever. Move the left-hand lever away from you, then push the one on the right. To lock the fortress into position, pull back the right lever, then the left, then listen for a noise. Push the right lever for different lengths of time, and you should be able to rotate the fortress fairly easily.

If you're having trouble, however, make *sure* you don't save the game and exit midway through any rotation. Restoring any games moves the fortress back to its initial position. On the other hand, if you're having trouble rotating the fortress and you already have the symbols you need, you can save your game, restore, and be in the position you need to complete the Age. It's practically the only time the wacky save-game feature is any help for the player.

Once you have all four symbols and have—by whatever method—moved the fortress back into its initial position, you're ready to leave. Enter the four symbols into the machine, and the floor of the short metal platform drops, revealing a secret chamber. The Myst book is inside.

— The Pages —

The story unfolds a little more when you return the red and blue pages to their books in the Myst Island library. The reception of your conversations seems to improve with every page you return. Sirrus tries to impress upon you the urgency of returning pages to him. "…must continue…don't waste time." He also tries to tell you something about Achenar: "…distorted mind…thirst for destruction." He promises you will be "greatly rewarded" if you help, he says, for it "is *I* who is wrongfully imprisoned."

Achenar doesn't waste any time trying to implicate Sirrus in his father's disappearance: "…hideously murdered our father…." He says that the blue pages are his only hope, since Sirrus's "greed is endless." While he wants you to continue to bring him pages ("You must obey me!"), he warns you against returning red pages to Sirrus.

Quick Fix for Tricky Bits

I can't get access to the clock tower. What do the wheels on shore do?

The designers have played a trick on you here because you can't see the effect the control wheels have on the clock in a single screen. Move a wheel, then look back up at the clock. You'll see that one of the clock hands has moved by one number. The big wheel controls the big hand, and the little wheel controls the little hand. Move the wheels until the clock reads 2:40. Push the control button, and a bridge then appears that leads to the clock tower.

What am I supposed to do in the elevator room in the fortress?

If you've taken the elevator to the top and exited the elevator, look up—there's some type of control on top of the elevator car. Go back inside the elevator and press the rectangular button between the up and down arrows. A noise alerts you that something's going on. Leave the elevator immediately, and the car drops down, making the controls accessible.

I can't rotate the fortress! Do the shadows or the cogs in the machinery mean anything?

You can learn to rotate the fortress in one of two ways—by practicing on the holographic imager in Achenar's room or by trial and error. Either way, the actual machinery doesn't provide any clues. The key is the amount of time you hold down the right-hand lever. The fortress can rotate at four points: north, east, west, and south. Each one of them has a different sound. So move the left lever away from you, then push the right-hand lever.

If you hear a "swoosh" noise like doors opening on a spaceship, you've rotated to the dead-end ocean position. A "dink" like a service bell gives you the first two digits of the code you need. A "dwip" sort of sloshy noise gives you the last two digits. And a "clang" like a spoon hitting a pot bottom means the fortress has rotated to its initial position, back to the cog wheel.

Chapter 6

Selenitic Age

Atrus initially described the Everdunes, or the Selenitic Age, as green and grassy, with fields, scattered forests, and a lake. A constant hot breeze from the north bathed the island.

But one night he was awakened from a sound sleep by what seemed to be a volcano. Explosions rocked the Everdunes, and gigantic balls of fire fell all around him. He beat a hasty retreat through one of the Myst books.

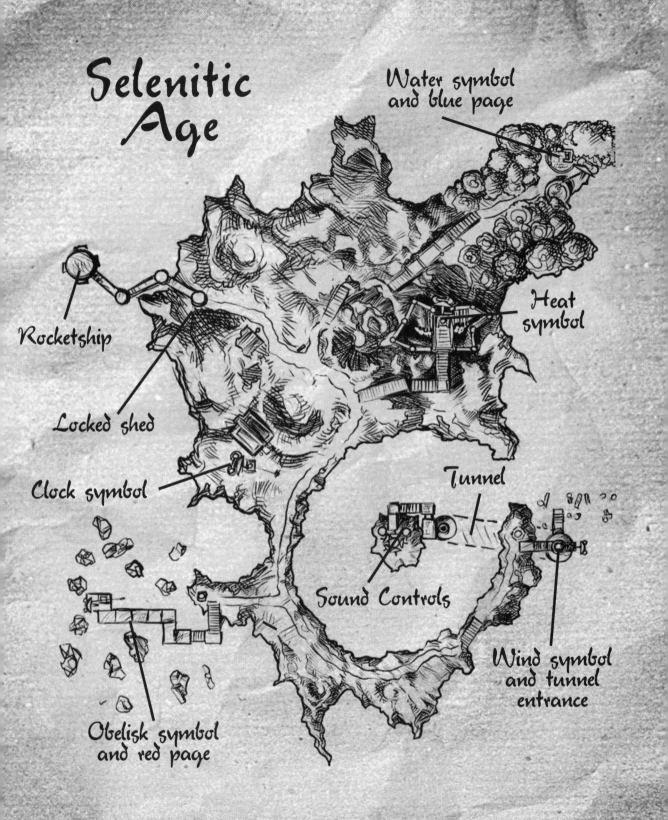

Selenitic Age

Water symbol and blue page

Rocketship

Heat symbol

Locked shed

Clock symbol

Tunnel

Sound Controls

Wind symbol and tunnel entrance

Obelisk symbol and red page

When he returned to the Everdunes, the island had turned into a desert, with gigantic craters marking the landscape. The only area that escaped the inferno was the knoll on which he had been sleeping when the first explosions hit. The hot northern wind was now nothing more than a pleasant breeze, and the original lake had dried up, only to be replaced by a larger body of water evidently created by a large meteor. Atrus said the noises from every corner of the island were constant, but not unpleasant.

During his stay Atrus was again jerked from a sound sleep—the hot breeze had returned, and with a low roar, the ground began to split open. A chasm opened; the heat was intense. But the ever-resourceful Atrus looked for a way to harness the heat, and in his exploration, he uncovered an underground cave system rich with raw materials.

Oddly, Atrus's journal entries fade in and out in this volume, much the way the Channelwood accounts change color from time to time.

— Getting There —

The mention of power sources and the drawing of the organ keys in Atrus's journal tell you how to start your travels to the Selenitic Age. Do your tower thing and stop the rotation on the rocketship. Your "Key" ladder clue is 59 volts. There's only one source of real power on Myst Island, so take off for the generator shed.

Go back down the stairs in the shed and take another look at the generator control panel. Now look behind you at the notice by the door. You can see that the meter on the left tells you the power produced by the generator, and the gauge on the right indicates the amount of power going to the rocketship.

The reason you have these different indicators is that it's possible to blow one of the breaker switches leading from the shed to the rocketship. So if you've been playing around with the power switches and all of a sudden the right-hand meter falls to zero while the one on the left keeps building power, you need to do a little repair work.

The breaker switch by the generator shed

There are two electrical towers leading to the rocketship, and both are easily accessible. One is just to the right and through the trees as you're going into the generator shed. The second is midway between the generator shed and the rocket. If you've blown a circuit, climb up the ladder to the top of one of the towers and see whether the switch has been tripped. Reset it if necessary and return to the power room; move to the next tower if the switch hasn't been tripped.

The breaker switch near the rocketship

Back down in the power room, try out all the switches by the power meters—but do it one by one and note the volts each one delivers.

switch no.	volts
1	10 volts
2	7 volts
3	8 volts
4	16 volts
5	5 volts
6	1 volt
7	2 volts
8	22 volts
9	19 volts
10	9 volts

There are lots of ways to deliver the required 59 volts to the rocketship. The easiest is by pressing buttons 4, 7, 8, and 9.

Once the 59 volts are humming through the power lines, go to the rocketship and walk inside. Fortify yourself; this can be the most difficult part of

the game if you don't have a very good ear. You might want to enlist someone's help during this puzzle, too—four ears are better than two.

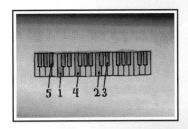

What you must do to travel to the Selenitic Age is match the notes in Atrus's journal with the sliding levers at the front of the rocketship. This ordinarily would just be a case of trial and error except for two things. First of all, the organ is at the opposite end of the rocket from the power levers. This means you must play a note and hum it or keep it in your head long enough to walk across the ship and try to match it on the slide bars. The other problem—and be very careful about this—is that once you've matched a note you can't touch that lever again. If you click on it, even by accident, the interface automatically turns to a "pull" icon, and the lever is jarred off one note and onto another.

If you're just hopeless at music and no virtuoso is handy, you can try counting the steps between the notes on the organ, then matching the number of steps with the levers. This is a crude method at best, but it can put you in the right ballpark. Regardless of how you manage to finish this puzzle, make sure you save your game the minute it's correct. There's no use risking a power outage and having to do it all over again. One way or another, once the puzzle's complete, you're off to the Selenitic Age.

— Take a Look Around —

The Everdunes is a gorgeous, restful place. You can hear the breeze and the water lapping against the shore, and the sun is shining through the fog that covers the island. A causeway leads from the rocket to the tall dunes that mark the paths here. The first structure you see is a door built into the side of a hill. It's locked, and the solution to entering would seem to lie with a switch to the right. When you pull the slide bars on the switch, you hear different sounds—roaring trains, water dripping, and so on. When you push the control button for the switch, you hear the sounds at which you've set the levers, but the door doesn't budge.

As you follow the path around the edge of the lake, you can see a large formation off to your right that's seemingly inaccessible. And as you explore the rest of the island, you see several strange structures scattered here and there. Brick staircases lead to altars of some kind, each of which has a different symbol mounted on it. There is also an old-fashioned microphone hanging somewhere near each of these "altars."

If you follow the path around the edge of the lake, you eventually come to a final podium, and this one has a tunnel that leads to the structure you saw from the mainland. Open the metal doors in front of you to reveal an odd machine made up of a view screen you can rotate to see the entire island, a series of five buttons with symbols on them, and a meter into which you're evidently supposed to enter sound frequencies. At least, that's what you can assume from the sonar dishes and antenna littering the place.

─Getting Down to Business─

From your starting point at the rocketship, walk forward until you pass the locked shed, then take a hard left so you end up on a hill sheltered by some trees. A small well is located to one side. Climb the stairs and move toward the "altar." The symbol here is of droplets of water falling into an ocean. Push the red button and watch the color of the symbol change. You might notice that an indicator light on the microphone behind you turns red.

And don't leave without either taking the blue page, located to the left of the altar, or noting its location and coming back for it later.

Go back down the hill in the direction of the locked shed. You'll see another brick staircase to your left. As you climb the winding stairs, you hear the bubble and hiss of lava. If you look over the sides of the barricades, you can see flame and smoke as well. This, then, is the chasm about which Atrus wrote. The altar here has a heat-wave symbol rising above a rift. Press the button and return to the main path.

The ruins of a clock tower are located just beyond where the walkway branches to the chasm. Its symbol is a pair of clock hands. Push the button, then continue past its broken gears.

After a bit the tall dunes and trees give way to a bare beach. When the path intersects, go to the right and follow a stairway that leads right over the water. Tall columns of stone jut from the water on all sides of the walkway. At the end of the path, you see another altar and a musical sound that can best be described as coming from a low-pitched pan flute. The symbol mounted on this podium is an obelisk patterned after the towers of rock around you. On top of the altar is Sirrus's red page.

Push the red button, then backtrack to the point at which the road intersects and continue on the main path. Follow it to the very tip of the island. Here is the fifth and final altar, where the sound of wind buffets all around you. A tunnel leads straight down, but luckily there's a ladder for you to climb. The symbol on this podium accurately reflects the scene—it's gusts of wind escaping a tunnel. Push this final button, then climb down the ladder.

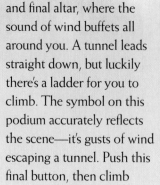

Turn on the light at the bottom of the ladder and travel through the tunnel, which goes under the water and to the structure you've seen from shore. Now that you've explored the island, you have a better idea of what that machine is for. Push one of the symbol buttons, then use the indicator arrows to move the view screen around the island. You can't help but notice that as you approach the site of one of the altars, the static noise in the reception is joined by whatever noise dominated at that site. For example, push the clock tower symbol. As you begin to see the clock tower in the view screen, you can also hear the ticking and tocking of its gears. Since the arrow keys begin flashing whenever you're close to a site, you can locate the five altars without much trouble.

But *finding* the altars is only half the battle. You need to tune in the noise perfectly so that there's no static. This means you must get the frequency to the nearest tenth, not just to the nearest number or two. Using your old friends, trial and error, you can arrive at the following solution:

water/well	153.4
heat/chasm	130.3
gears/clock	55.6
flute/obelisk	15.0
wind/tunnel	212.2

When the final frequency has been entered, press the control button—the buttons flash in a new pattern: flute, water, wind, heat, gears. Now you have the "key" to the locked shed.

Return to the shed and move the sliders until each one is tuned to the sound in the pattern. Push the control button, and the door slides open.

Follow the corridor down and you eventually reach a room with a tiny H.G. Wells–type vehicle. This is the tram car that can take you through Atrus's underground cave system. Push the button to open its door, then climb into the pilot's chair.

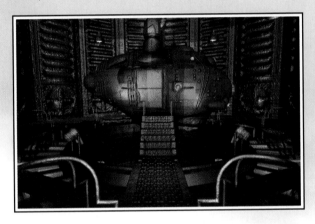

Controlling the tram car isn't as difficult as it initially seems, especially if you've recently played through the Mechanical Age. The tracks are extremely complex, and they move in eight different directions: north, northeast, east, southeast, south, southwest, west, and northwest. That's the bad news. The good news is that the tram car actually tells you which direction to go, using the same noises (with east and west switched) you heard when you rotated the fortress. Remember:

north = service bell "dink"

east = spaceship doors "swoosh"

south = spoon hitting pot "clang"

west = squishy "dwip"

If you need to move between two major compass points, such as to the northeast or southwest, you hear a combination of the two noises—a "swoosh-dink" or "dwip-clang." A general rule if you're trying to play through the game on your own is that when you're in doubt, rotate to the right. There are only three counterclockwise rotations in the 13 moves.

Push the forward bar to move the tram onto the tracks, then listen for the noise it makes as it finishes the rotation. "Dink!" Your first move should be to the north. The backtrack bar is obviously to retrace your steps if you've made a wrong turn. The arrow keys rotate the car from track to track, as indicated by the window on the right. You can proceed down a track as long as it's clear. For example, the tram stops at an intersection in the track. If there's a red light in front of you when it stops, this means the track doesn't continue forward and you need to choose a different direction.

There's also a little bug near the end on the MPC version of *Myst* that can flip the direction-indicator window from North to East. Don't be fooled—just go ahead and rotate the tram to Southeast, the final direction of your trip.

Warning!

The train trip is another notorious slowdown section. If your system is prone to problems elsewhere in the game, you need to save your game before you start going through the tunnels, quit the program, then restore the saved game. If you get to the middle of the route and start having access-time problems, it's still going to be faster to exit and start over than to try to make it through to the end. It's experience talkin', folks.

You know your train has arrived, so to speak, when you see a big metal door in front of you instead of track or a red stoplight. Hop out of the tram and through the door, then grab the Myst book for a hasty retreat. Be sure to save your game as soon as you get back in the library. You must complete the track one more time to pick up the second page, but there's no point in risking having to do it a *third* time.

Double Warning!!

It's a nasty blow that the Zip Mode interface has no effect on the tram travel. This means that when you return to the Selenitic Age for the second page, you're going to have to go all the way through the caves again. Be sure to write down the path you take if you're trying to play the game on your own. Otherwise, follow this path: N, W, N, E, E, S, S, W, SW, W, NW, NE, N, SE.

— The Pages —

The conversations with Sirrus and Achenar are clearer than ever as you return the fourth pages of their books. But you certainly don't have a clearer view of what happened to trap the brothers inside these books.

Sirrus again warns you against the "demented" Achenar and promises to reward you if you return more pages to him. Achenar, he says, "took advantage of the freedom.... He will destroy both myself and you." As a parting shot, he says earnestly, "I am innocent and he is guilty."

Achenar, on the other hand, is "convinced that Sirrus is guilty." He is an "innocent bystander" who was "wrongly tricked." He tells you that Sirrus deceived Atrus and convinced his father that Achenar was responsible for some unnamed horror. Again, he warns you about Sirrus's "unbridled lust for riches."

Quick Fix for Tricky Bits

One of the power meters in the generator shed won't move off "00." What's the deal?

You've overloaded the system and tripped a circuit breaker. Climb up one of the two electrical towers—one down a hill by the generator shed, the other closer to the rocket—and flip the tripped switch. Then be careful not to let it happen again as you experiment with the voltage buttons.

I can't get the slide bars in the rocketship to play the correct tune!

If you don't have a good ear, this one is really tough. You can, however, get in the general vicinity by counting notes from the bottom of the organ keyboard and the bottom of the slider and trying to match them up. It's not a perfect method, but it's a start.

I've tuned in sound frequencies, but nothing happens when I push the control button. What am I doing wrong?

One of your frequencies probably isn't precisely right. You need to hear the correct tone without any static whatsoever. Here are the frequencies:

water/well	153.4
heat/chasm	130.3
gears/clock	55.6
flute/obelisk	15.0
wind/tunnel	212.2

What's the directional path I should take through the subway?

Follow this path: N, W, N, E, E, S, S, W, SW, W, NW, NE, N, SE.

Chapter 7

Stoneship Age

Atrus writes that when he first traveled to the Stoneship Age, the sole inhabitant of The Rocks was a boy named Emmit. He lived alone on this cluster of rocks, but soon another boy appeared from the sea whom Emmit named Branch. The two new friends lived in caves on the largest rock. It was an idyllic island where the sun always shone and the water was always clear. The weather was temperate, with a breeze from the north.

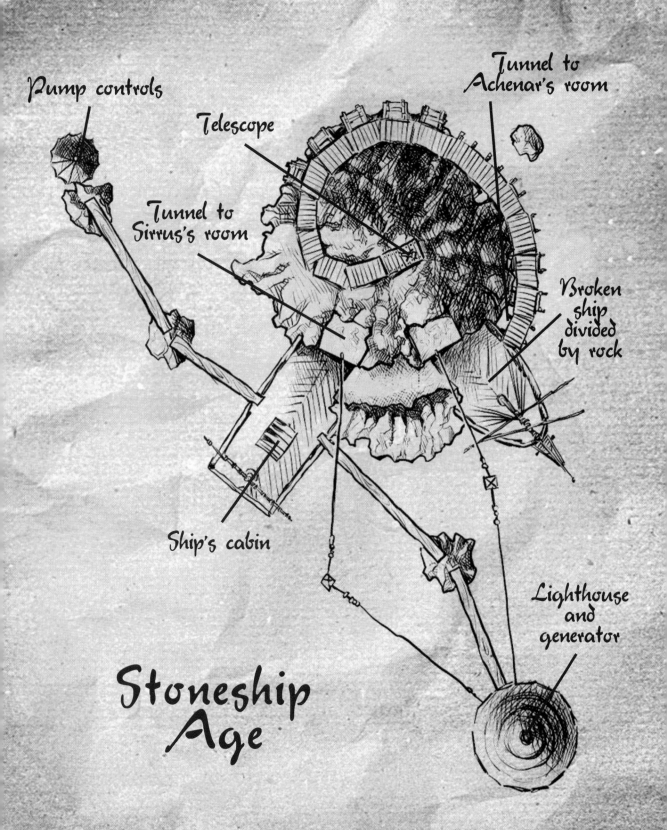

Pump controls

Telescope

Tunnel to
Achenar's room

Tunnel to
Sirrus's room

Broken
ship
divided
by rock

Ship's cabin

Lighthouse
and
generator

Stoneship
Age

In time, another boy was found swimming near The Rocks. This boy was named Will. Soon after Will's appearance, it began to rain—an occurrence that scared the boys because they had never seen it.

Atrus, meanwhile, was working on The Art, a practice that enabled him to create things simply by writing about them in his journals. He created a ship, but when it appeared, it was cut in half by one of the rocks. Atrus was also studying the stars in the area and naming the constellations. He could see a light in the distance that was no star. He assumed there was a nearby land, explaining the appearances of Emmit, Branch, and Will.

One day an actual storm struck The Rocks, with heavy rain, thunder, and lightning. Shortly afterward, Atrus began plans to build a lighthouse run by a generator to signal any nearby islands. The scheme worked, and a girl and man arrived not long after the lighthouse was completed.

Atrus left the Stoneship Age for ten years, and when he returned, the boys he had known had turned into men. There were also many new inhabitants on The Rocks, and someone had evidently discovered gold on the island. It had not rained, however, for seven years. The only other difference Atrus noticed was that the rock on which they had built the lighthouse was slowly sinking into the ocean.

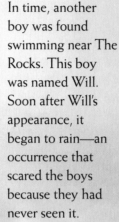

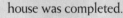

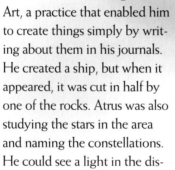

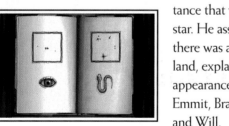

— Getting There —

Mentions of ships and constellations are enough to put you on the trail of the Stoneship Age. The tower rotation provides you with three clues:

October 11, 1984, 10:04 a.m.

January 17, 1207, 5:46 a.m.

November 23, 9791, 6:57 p.m.

Since the constellations from the Stoneship Age are the same symbols as those mounted on the pillars surrounding the fountains, go there and find the three you need: leaf, snake, and insect. Press the symbols so each changes color; then stand back. You'll see that the sunken ship in the fountain has now risen to the surface.

Go to the planetarium and lie back in the chair. Be sure to turn off the lights before you relax. Pull down the overhead gear and move the sliding levers so one of the dates matches a tower rotation clue. Push the control button, and a constellation comes into view. Match it with one of those drawn in Atrus's journal, then find the constellations for the other two dates.

A quick trip to the dock reveals that the sunken ship there, too, has now surfaced. Go through a door on deck to find the Myst book that takes you to the Stoneship Age, the area most like a traditional graphic adventure in all of *Myst*.

You arrive in the Stoneship Age on the deck of the ship Atrus created with The Art. A large rock separates one part of the ship from the other; a door leads into the rock from both decks. The corridors beyond these doors are dark, although you can see light fixtures mounted on the walls. They're also impassable because they're filled with water. The door leading down to the Myst book is also filled with water.

There's not much to see in this Age. To one side a wooden causeway leads to three large buttons covered by an umbrella. You hear machinery grind into action when you push the buttons. A walkway in the opposite direction leads to a three-story lighthouse now filled with water up to the second-level floor. A key is bolted to the floor in front of you. There's also a locked trap door in the ceiling.

Back on the deck of the ship, you see a wooden path leading up the craggy face of the rock. At the top of this steep climb, however, you see nothing but a telescope. You can't see much more than empty sea as you scan the horizon, although the top of the light-house comes into view. You've seen that view before in Atrus's journal.

Getting Down to Business

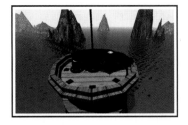

Move from the deck of the ship down the walkway toward the umbrella-covered buttons. These are the drainage controls; each one drains a different area on The Rocks. Push the one on the right to pump the water out of the lighthouse, then move back across to that structure.

With the water gone, you see a circular staircase in the lighthouse leading down. Follow it to the base of the lighthouse—there's a locked chest down there. If you look at the chest very carefully, you see a small valve on the bottom. Turn the valve to drain the water from the chest, then close it again.

Now return to the drainage controls and press the middle button. Go back to the lighthouse. The water has returned, but now the buoyant chest has bobbed to the surface, conveniently located near the key bolted to the floor.

Open the chest and take out the key inside. Climb the ladder and unlock the trap door; then go up into the dome of the lighthouse.

Once you've enjoyed the fantastic view from the top of the lighthouse, take a look at the generator. The controls here are easy—a crank that powers up a battery pack. Take a look at the battery gauge; the solid gray bar indicates that the batteries are totally drained. Turn the crank until the gauge is solid white, then leave the lighthouse. You get around ten minutes of power from each full gauge, so plan your exploring accordingly, and recharge the generator when necessary.

Since you've already drained the tunnels, go do some exploring now that the lights are on. Follow a steep staircase down until you reach a door. Press the button in the center of the door and step inside one of the brothers' bedrooms.

As always, you learn more about Sirrus and Achenar by exploring their surroundings. And what you learn is, as always, disturbing. Sirrus's bedroom is exotic, with heavy wood furniture and rich carpeting. A desk drawer reveals drug paraphernalia—needles and vials. When you go through the drawers on the tall cabinet along one wall, you find coins, fabrics…and a red page in the bottom drawer.

Achenar's bedroom is far removed from Sirrus's. The furnishings are crude, and antlers and bony stuff hang on the walls. There's a blue page on top of the stained bedlinens.

A holographic device sits on top of his chest of drawers. When you activate it, you get a lovely three-dimensional rose that morphs into a human skull. Creepy! The drawers are filled with maps, but there's a torn note in the bottom drawer that is obviously the other half of the note you found in Channelwood.

Putting the two pieces together, you reconstruct the message:

Marker Switch Vault Access
Island of Myst

The vault is located in very plain view on the Island of Myst, and access can be achieved very easily if the simple instructions are followed. First, locate each of the Marker Switches on the island. Turn every one of these switches to the "on" position. Then go to the dock and, as a final step, turn the Marker Switch there to the "off" position.

People playing the MPC version should again be aware that this version of Myst has a typographical error in this note. Replace the first "off" with the word "on" so it matches the note shown here.

Well, you've explored all of The Rocks, and you still don't have any idea how to get back to Myst Island. If you drain the room where the Myst book is, you just end up stumbling around in the dark; evidently the generator doesn't power this area of the island. You must be missing something. And since there were connecting passageways between the brothers' rooms in the Mechanical Age, maybe you should look for something of that sort here.

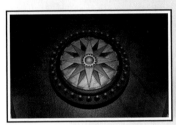

Drain the tunnels again and take a closer look as you go down either corridor. At one point a red square marks a small panel on the wall. Push the panel to reveal another tunnel.

In the center of the tunnel is an enormous compass wheel edged by a circle of buttons. When you push one of the buttons, the lights go out, and you must find your way back to the ship's deck by the flash of a warning light.

Power up the generator again and go up to the telescope on the summit of The Rocks. This time when you adjust the view screen, the top of the lighthouse comes into view with its shining beacon. Since it's still the only thing of note in sight, go ahead and mark the position of the light.

Return to the compass room in the secret passageway and observe the 32 buttons around the circumference of the wheel. Since there are 360 degrees in a circle,

each button represents 11.25 degrees. The lighthouse beacon came into view at 135 degrees. Grab a calculator or pull out that *Myst Journal* for a little 'rithmetic, and you'll figure out that the twelfth button (clockwise, of course) marks the 135-degree mark. Give a quick push, and the entire wheel bursts into light.

Now you're set, so leave the tunnels and use the left-hand drainage control to empty the water from the cabin on the ship's deck. Walk through the lush wooden interior and down the stairs. Move toward a plain wooden table and touch it. A Myst book magically emerges from its surface. Open it up, and you're on your way back to Myst Island.

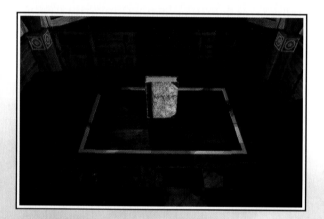

⌐ The Pages ⌐

You get more than you bargain for when you return the fifth pages to the brothers' books. This time around, they tell you the secrets of the fireplace in the library. Evidently there's still another page for each book in a secret room accessed from that hearth. There's also a mysterious green book they both warn you not to open. The key to the fireplace is the puzzle book from the bookcase. Go to puzzle 158 and enter the design on the metal grid on the door of the fireplace. Oh, yeah—each brother also (1) proclaimed he was innocent and (2) accused his brother of guilt.

Quick Fix for Tricky Bits

Where am I supposed to use the tower clues?

Enter the three dates on the control grid above the chair in the planetarium. Make sure you've turned out the lights first, however, or you won't see any of the constellations.

I can't identify the constellations. What are they?

The three constellations are the leaf, the snake, and the insect.

I can't go anywhere on The Rocks! Everything's covered with water.

The drainage controls for the flooded areas of The Rocks are under the umbrella. The left button pumps out the ship's cabin; the middle one, the tunnels cut into the rock; and the right button, the lighthouse.

How do I get the chest up so the bolted key can open it?

There's a small valve on the visible short side of the chest. Open the valve to drain the chest, but make sure you close it again to make it watertight. When you flood the lighthouse again, the chest floats to the surface of the water.

I've searched the brothers' rooms, but I still don't have any clue how to get back to Myst Island. What am I missing?

There's a secret passage on the stairways leading down to the brothers' rooms. Look for a panel marked by a red square. Push the panel to gain access to the all-important compass room.

What's the deal with the compass wheel? Every time I push a button, the lights go out.

There's only one button you can push on the wheel without sucking all the power from the generator. If you've looked through the telescope, you've seen the beacon at the top of the lighthouse shining at 135 degrees. On the compass wheel, 135 degrees is marked at button number 12. Give 'er a push.

Chapter 8

Conclusion

You've now got all the pieces to the puzzle that make up *Myst*. All you have to do is put them together. And the first place to start is, naturally enough, with the puzzle book. Pull it off the shelf and turn to puzzle 158.

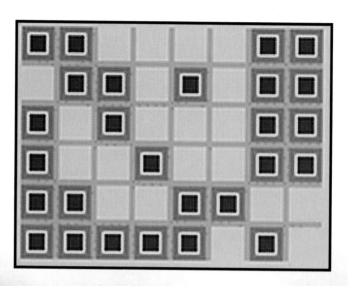

— The Fireplace —

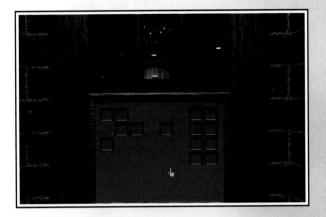

Since neither brother has ever done anything to make you trust him, pull down the green book and open it. Here, it seems, is Atrus. Father, unlike sons, seems rational and wise. He tells you that he is trapped in a place called Dunny and that the books he writes, like his father's before him, transport him to new worlds. The red and blue books were written to trap people who might have ulterior motives in mind, but he never expected to catch his own sons.

Atrus, too, has a page he wishes you to deliver to him. If you bring him a white page (please don't ask why it's not green) for his Myst book, he can travel again. Are you up to the challenge?

Step into the fireplace and push the button to close the door. The closed door is metal, and you can touch it wherever you wish to raise a pattern of squares. Follow the pattern in the puzzle book, then push the button again when it's complete.

If you've entered the pattern correctly, the fireplace rotates to reveal a small room. Shelves reveal final red and blue pages and a green Myst book that matches that of Sirrus and Achenar.

‒ The White Page ‒

The torn note you retrieved from the Channelwood and Stoneship Ages is the key to finding the white page. The message is fairly clear: a secret vault will be uncovered if you turn on all the marker switches, then turn off the one on the dock.

Rotate the fireplace back to the library, and if you need to, double-check the Myst Island map to make sure all the master switches are still turned on. Then zip out to the dock and turn off the master switch there. *Voila!* A panel opens in the base of the switch—the white page is inside.

Take the white page back into the fireplace. You'll have to enter the pattern again to rotate to the greenbook room. Atrus is waiting and once again asking about the white page. Once you have it, you can touch the book and be transported to Dunny.

‒ Dunny ‒

The area where Atrus has spent his imprisonment seems calm and scholarly, not unlike the man himself. It looks like a stone cave, yet there's a mosaic on the floor, and several doors lead away from the great room. Atrus is hard at work in a far corner at a desk surrounded by books and papers. You try to explore, but you don't make much progress.

As you approach Atrus at his desk, he holds out his hand for the white page and takes it (in a neat bit of animation). He then abruptly leaves to take care of his sons, although he promises to return soon.

You try again to explore while Atrus is gone, but again with no luck. Atrus eventually returns, having dispensed with his sons,

although he worries that his time spent imprisoned has had a devastating effect on his writing and on the fate of his wife. "I'm fighting a foe much greater than my sons could even imagine," he tells you.

As a final word, he gives you permission to explore Myst Island and its lands at your leisure…although he may need your help again. You return to the library with the Myst book on his desk. There you get a hint about the brothers' fate, but the entire ending is very ambiguous. Hmmm. Stay tuned for the sequel, folks—you've solved the first secret of *Myst*.

— That Other Option —

You had to have wondered, even if you resisted temptation like a good little adventurer. What would happen if you did free one of the brothers? Would you actually have learned what was going on in *Myst*? Would you get clues to the plot of *Myst II*?

Unfortunately, bad deeds are even less often rewarded in graphic adventures than they are in real life. No sooner do you return the final page to one of the books than you get an up-close-and-personal look at imprisonment yourself. Your viewpoint changes, and suddenly you see the former prisoner standing in the library while you are inside the books. Gleefully, the brother begins pulling out pages from your book, and the conversation becomes more filled with static until….

Chapter 9

The "You're-No-Adventurer-You're-a-Cheat" Walk-Thru

Proceed at your own risk. This chapter contains a no-frills walk-thru of all of *Myst*. No challenge. No surprises. So if you want to impress your friends with your gaming prowess, don't peek at this chapter.

— Myst Island —

From your starting place on the dock, walk straight ahead and up the stairs. Move toward the library and pick up Atrus's note. Since he mentions the fore-chamber, return to the dock and take the small door cut into the side of the island. Go inside and click on the cauldron button. There's a note by the door with the correct settings for this Dimensional Imager.

Press the tiny green button to the left, open the control panel, and enter the number settings. In addition to the pool at which the imager is presently set, you can get a topographical map of Myst Island and a holographic image of the marker switches. Since the note you found on the grass told you to count the marker switches, explore the island, turning on the switches (you can't yet reach the one by the clock tower) and counting them. There are eight in all:

- **The dock**

- **The giant cog wheel**

- **The planetarium**

- **The rocketship**

- **The fountain**

- **The generator shed**

- **The cabin**

- **The clock tower**

Return to the fore-chamber and enter the number of switches into the Dimensional Imager. You get your first message from Atrus, in which he speaks to his wife, Catherine, of his suspicions about their sons, and the "tower rotation."

Once the message is completed, go to the library. You can do some research for your travels by reading Atrus's journals—they're among the burned books on the bookshelf. You can also hear from the brothers themselves by returning the first red and blue pages to the books.

As you approach the map of Myst Island, landmarks appear on its surface. This is what turning on the master switches accomplished; if any are missing, you may have missed a switch. The round tower behind the library is blinking. Click on it and hold until an indicator line leading from it begins to rotate around the island. The line turns red at four locations: the giant cog, the ship, the giant tree behind the cabin, and the rocketship. Stop the line at the tree/cabin. As you release the tower, you hear the grinding of heavy machinery.

Now go to the painting of the open bookcase. Click on it—the entrance to the library closes, but a secret passageway behind the bookshelf is revealed. Follow the corridor to an elevator, and take the elevator to the tower.

As the doors of the elevator open, you face a ladder with a book emblem mounted on it. Climb the ladder and look through the slit window at the top. You should see the giant tree. Climb back down, but instead of getting in the elevator, go behind it. There's another ladder there, this one with a key emblem. A metal plate is attached to the wall. On it is written "7, 2, 4." Repeat the tower rotation until you have all four clues:

Tree:	7, 2, 4
Giant cog:	2:40 2, 2, 1
Rocketship:	59 volts
Sunken ship:	October 11, 1984, 10:04 a.m. January 17, 1207, 5:46 a.m. November 23, 9791, 6:57 p.m.

‒ Channelwood Age ‒

To get to the Channelwood Age, go to the cabin and enter the tower clue—7, 2, 4—as the combination to the safe. There's a box of matches inside. Strike a match, then move to the furnace at the other end of the room. The pilot light is in the bottom left-hand corner. Touch it with the match. Now move to the fuel wheel to the right. Turn it clockwise as far as it will go. The banging you hear outside is the elevator car moving up the trunk of the giant tree.

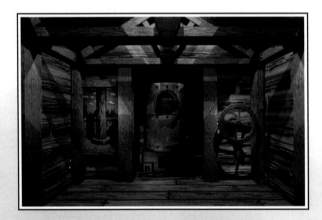

When the noise stops, turn off the fuel wheel and run outside. You should be able to get inside the elevator car before it goes back underground. If not, repeat the steps until you can step into the car. The elevator takes you to a hidden room; the Myst book is inside.

Once you're in the Channelwood Age, move left until you reach a windmill. Go inside and turn on the faucet at the base of the large tank. Back on the walkways, adjust the switches controlling the water flow so the plain elevator (not the one by the spiral staircase) gets water pressure. Take the elevator up one level.

Search the huts until you find a lever under a window that overlooks the circular staircase. Pull the lever so the locked wooden door to the stairs opens. Leave that hut and move to the right until you reach the elevator and staircase. Take the stairs down and reroute the water so it reaches the elevator. Climb back up and take the elevator to the third level.

Search Achenar's and Sirrus's rooms until you find the red and blue pages. (The red page is in Sirrus's desk; the blue page is on the floor next to Achenar's video machine.) While you're in Sirrus's room, look in the right-hand drawer under his bed. Write down what you can read in the torn note.

Return to the ground level of Channelwood and look for an elevator that lies just beyond a gap in the walkway on one path and a gap in the pipeline on another. Switch the direction of the water so it's headed toward the gap in the walkway, then pull the lever that's there. A hidden bridge is revealed. Walk along it past the elevator and turn a crank to extend the pipeline across the gap. Retrace your steps and reroute the water a final time so it's flowing through the pipe. Now that the elevator has power, take it up one floor to a hidden room with a Myst book that carries you back to Myst Island.

Return whichever page you brought back with you to its proper book, then return to Channelwood, reroute water until you can pick up the other page, and return it, too. This goes for all the Ages.

Mechanical Age

The tower clue for the giant cog is the key to the Mechanical Age: 2:40 and 2-2-1.

Go to the clock tower and look at the wheels on shore. Each time you click on one, it moves a hand of the clock on the tower. Move the little wheel until the little hand points to 2 and the big wheel until the big hand points to 8. A hidden bridge rises from the water. Cross the bridge and go inside the clock tower—and don't forget to turn on the final master switch by the door.

The machine inside has three dials on top reading 3-3-3 and a lever on either side. Pull and release the left lever so the numbers move to 3-1-1. Pull and release the right lever so the numbers read 1-2-1. Now pull and hold the right lever. The top number jumps to 2; keep holding until the middle number clicks to 2 as well. When you have the 2-2-1 pattern, the cog at the base of the machine opens, and so does the giant cog on Myst Island. Go to the giant cog and travel with the Myst book inside to the Mechanical Age.

The Mechanical Age is like a bike wheel: you need to rotate the center to different spokes before you can leave. The machine on the rock where you arrive requires four symbols to work. You get those symbols in two different locations you can access only by rotating the entire central fortress.

But before you get to all that, go into the fortress and search the brothers' rooms. There's a secret passage in each—behind the tapestry in Sirrus's room and between the throne and the rotation imager in Achenar's. The red and blue pages are inside the hidden rooms.

Once you've explored both rooms and both secret passages, move to the hall that connects the brothers' rooms. Push the red button to access the stairway down. Pull the lever on the machine down there until the circle indicators match up and turn red. Go back upstairs and push the red button. Cross the short hallway to the elevator and take it up one floor.

Once you've reached the tower room, press the rectangular button between the up and down arrows in the elevator car, then step immediately from the elevator. The car drops down far enough to reveal some controls. This is how you rotate the fortress.

You can rotate the fortress in four directions, although one is a dead end. You can tell when you've successfully hit a position by the noise you hear:

north = service bell "dink"
(first two symbols)

east = squishy "dwip"
(last two symbols)

south = spoon hitting pot "clang"
(initial position/exit)

west = spaceship doors "swoosh"
(dead end)

To rotate the fortress, push the left-hand lever and leave it. Push the right-hand lever for a certain amount of time, pull it back, then pull back the left-hand lever. If you hear a noise, you've hit one of the locations. If you hear nothing, you've rotated to an invalid position. Experiment with the length of time you push the right-hand lever until you hit the different spots.

Once you have all four symbols—a horseshoe, a triangle-rectangle-triangle, a moon over three trees, and a semicircle—a passageway opens down to a secret chamber containing the Myst book. Returning for the other page is a breeze.

— Selenitic Age —

Rotate the tower to the rocketship and pick up the "59 volts" clue. Then go to the generator shed and move downstairs to the power controls. Push the buttons until you have 59 volts powering through. (Buttons 4, 7, 8, and 9 is one way.) If the right-hand gauge drops to zero, go outside to one of the circuit breaker towers—just outside the shed or closer to the rocket—and reset the switch, then try again.

When you've set the correct voltage, go to the rocket and use the organ clue from the journal to set the sliding levers. Once the levers match the notes, you're off to the Selenitic Age.

On the Everdunes, look for five different brick structures, each with an "altar," a microphone, and a sound dish. Push the red button at the base of each symbol on each altar to activate the microphone. The water symbol (where the blue page can be located) is a hard left from the locked shed. The heat symbol is just to the left of the main path and the clock symbol is just to the right of the main path. The obelisk symbol (where the red page can be located) is to the right where the main path forks, and the wind symbol is to the left of the fork, on the far end of the island.

Once you've activated all five microphones, take the tunnel by the wind symbol down and and walk under the water to a small outcropping laden with machinery and sound dishes. You need to find the sound frequencies for each of the "altars" by adjusting the video screen and surveying the island for the noises produced by the microphones—you want a clear sound without any static. The correct frequencies are:

water/well	153.4
heat/chasm	130.3
gears/clock	55.6
flue/obelisk	15.0
wind/tunnel	212.2

When the final frequency has been entered, press the control button. The buttons flash in a new pattern: flue, water, wind, heat, gears. Now you have the "key" to the locked shed.

Return to the locked shed and move the sliders until each one is tuned to the sound in the pattern. Push the control button, and the door slides open. Go inside and follow the hallway until you reach a small tram. Climb into the pilot's seat to maneuver your way through the underground caverns. The direction in which you should go is indicated by the sound you hear at each stop. The sounds match the rotation directions from the Mechanical Age, except east and west are switched:

north	=	**service bell "dink"**
east	=	**spaceship doors "swoosh"**
south	=	**spoon hitting pot "clang"**
west	=	**squishy "dwip"**

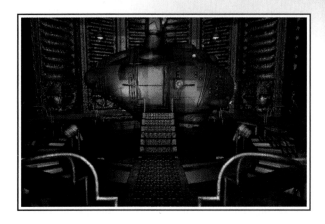

If you're supposed to go northeast, southeast, southwest, or northwest, you hear a combination of the two sounds that make up that direction. The correct path ends up being N, W, N, E, E, S, S, W, SW, W, NW, NE, N, and SE. There's a door in front of the final stop; exit the tram and find the Myst book so you can travel back to the main island. Unfortunately, when you return for the second page, you have to run the cavern maze again.

Stoneship Age

Rotate the tower to the sunken ship for the final clues:

October 11, 1984, 10:04 a.m.

January 17, 1207, 5:46 a.m.

November 23, 9791, 6:57 p.m.

Go into the planetarium, turn off the lights, and enter the three dates in the overhead gear. Match the constellations you see with the ones in Atrus's journal. You end up with the leaf, the snake, and the insect.

Head for the pillars surrounding the fountain and press the buttons on the three that match the constellations. The sunken ship in the fountain rises, and so does the ship by the dock. Go into the cabin of the ship and take the Myst book to The Rocks, the Stoneship Age.

Much of the Stoneship Age is underwater, but pumps are located at the end of a pier under an umbrella. The one on the left drains the ship's cabin, the one in the middle drains the tunnels in the big rock, and the one on the right drains the lighthouse. Press the right-hand button and go to the lighthouse.

Go down the lighthouse stairs and take a look at the chest there. Open the small valve and drain the water, then close the valve again. Flood the lighthouse again so the chest floats to the walkway and you can open it with the key bolted to the floor. Use the key inside the chest to open the trap door in the ceiling, then go into the dome of the lighthouse.

Crank the generator wheel at the far end of the room until the battery gauge shows solid white. Each charged battery gives you about ten minutes of power.

Drain the tunnels in the rock and search them. There's a bedroom at the bottom of each hallway. Look for a red page in the bottom drawer of the cabinet in Sirrus's room. There's a blue page on Achenar's bed, as well as the missing half of the torn note from Channelwood in the bottom drawer of his chest of drawers. There's a typographical error at this point in the MPC version of *Myst*. The word "off" should read "on."

On your way up either staircase, look for a panel marked with a red square. Press it to reveal a hidden passageway that leads to a compass wheel surrounded by buttons.

Go to the telescope on the summit of The Rocks and adjust it until the lighthouse beacon comes into view, as indicated by Atrus's journals. You spot the light at 135 degrees. When you return to the wheel, press the equivalent button (the 12th, clockwise). That turns on the light source for the ship's cabin.

Drain the cabin, then go down the stairs until you reach a table. Click on it and a Myst book emerges. You have to charge the generator and drain the tunnels again to pick up the page you left behind, but it's a fairly quick procedure.

— Conclusion —

When you return the fifth pages to the brothers, they tell you there's a final page for each of their books that can be found in a secret room accessed through the fireplace. Take out the puzzle book from the bookshelf and copy puzzle 158. Go into the fireplace, shut the door, and copy the pattern on the iron plate inset into the door. Press the elevator button to rotate the chamber.

Take it to Atrus and he transports you to Dunny, where you hand over the page in person. He disappears to take care of his deceitful sons. When he returns, he offers you a Myst book to continue your travels, starts planning a way to help his wife, and warns you that he might need your help in the future.

Congratulations—you've finished Myst!

There are red and blue pages in the secret room, but also a green Myst book. Open it, and Atrus asks you for a white page that releases him from the book.

Rotate the fireplace back into place and use the clues provided in the torn note to find the white page. First check the Myst Island map and make sure all the marker switches are on. Then go to the dock and turn off the switch there. A secret panel opens in the switch podium, with the white page inside.

Appendix A:
Troubleshooting for the Windows/MPC *Myst*

A four-page pamphlet that outlines a bunch of the what-can-go-wrong-will-go-wrong situations in *Myst* is included with every MPC *Myst*. But who wants to wade through all that technical-ese? Here are the major solutions the Brøderbund technical support staff offers to people having problems playing this version of *Myst*.

- Make sure you've updated your *Myst* program to version 1.01 (serial number 44962).

- Add or edit the OPTIMIZE= line in the video section of the QTW.INI file to OPTIMIZE=BMP. This file is located in the Windows directory.

- Disable your SMARTDRIVE program in either your CONFIG.SYS or AUTOEXEC.BAT file by placing a REM or ; (semicolon) command in front of the line and rebooting your system.

- Increasing your Virtual Memory swap file to 10,000 and keeping your Windows resources at 85 percent also helps.

- Here's the biggie: updating the device drivers for sound card, video card, and CD-ROM components resolves more than 90 percent of the problems people have with *Myst*. Hardware companies update these drivers at least every six months, and usually much more frequently. You can get the drivers directly from the makers of your computer components.

Appendix B:
Troubleshooting for the Macintosh *Myst*

Since *Myst* was designed for the Macintosh, people haven't been running into as many problems playing this version of the game. However, once again, these are solutions to the obstacles the technical support staff at Brøderbund finds are most often encountered:

🐦 Make sure you're using the 1.01 version of *Myst* (serial number 44602), and make sure you're using the *Myst* version of QuickTime to run the program.

🐦 If you're not, take the current version out of your extension folder, trash it, then empty the trash. Reboot your Mac, then put the *Myst* QuickTime into the folder. Also make sure you take all the extensions out of your Extensions folder—with the exception of Sound Manager, your CD-ROM extension, and the *Myst* version of QuickTime—and place them in your Disabled Extensions folder. Reboot your Mac to have them take effect.

🐦 Make sure you don't have any control panels activated that might act as extensions, especially the Modern Memory Manager. Check which ones are active as extensions by looking in the task list of your Mac. The Modern Memory Manager is used only on Power Macintoshes.

🐦 Disable the Power Plug control panel when running *Myst*. Again, it's used only on Power Macs.

🐦 Change your preferred memory size to either 5000K or 6000K. You should also make sure your Disk Cache is set to 128.

🐦 You should not be using any sort of auto-doubling or compression software with *Myst*.

Afterword:
Myst II and Beyond

Okay—now you've finished *Myst* and you're feeling a little empty, maybe even a little cheated. You still aren't entirely sure what was going on, and you don't know what's really happened to Sirrus, Achenar, Atrus, or even the camera-shy Catherine. How much longer do you have to wait for the story to continue? And what will that story be?

The hints are there that *Myst II* will center on Atrus's efforts to rescue Catherine from whatever place she's presently being held captive. That was confirmed by a Brøderbund employee who acted as though he were handing over state secrets to share even that much information. Here's what Rand Miller has to say about the sequel to the game he created with his brother, Robyn.

"There is a sequel in progress. It takes off where *Myst* left off—or left you hanging, in some people's opinion. It's not gonna take place on any of the places *Myst* did. It's gonna be larger and continue the story right where *Myst* left off! [*Myst* was] designed for a feeling [of isolation]—I think maybe it's too much. The next one may have some changes to make you feel more in touch."

And although Miller hinted that *Myst II* would have a shorter turn-around time than *Myst*'s two-year development, it doesn't look like that's going to be the case. *Myst* came out for Macintosh in September 1993; the Windows/MPC version followed in February 1994. But it doesn't look like *Myst II* will make it to stores during 1995, although our mole at Brøderbund says, "It would be a great Christmas present if it did."

So what's a gamer to do in the meantime? Well, you can wait for one of the other versions of *Myst* to be released and do some comparisons. Miller confirmed that *Myst* is on its way to more than one CD-based video-game system, although he griped about the slow process of trying to find the right people to do the job.

Those going through withdrawal can get some *Myst* background in the book project that's in the works. *Myst: The Blood of the Son* was purchased in the summer of 1994 by Hyperion for around $900,000. A three-book set is expected. You can also hang around your local theatre and wait for the *Myst* movie that has been optioned by Disney. Given the production time of a film, it's not inconceivable that the movie and the sequel game will hit simultaneously.

But why should you wait? You've seen what the game's graphics look like. Are there going to be that many surprises in *Myst II*? Miller promises that there will be, and he's looking forward to squashing even more technology into the second game.

"The future looks incredible," he says. "I think we're only scratching the surface of what interactive gaming will be in the near future. The combination of new hardware and software makes for a fantastic turn of events. We had to hold back in *Myst* for compatibility things, but I think we'll have to do less of that—even on the sequel, we're designing things that will raise the bar."